Contents

Beef & Bean Burritos

Makes 8 burritos

Prep Time: 5 minutes   Cook Time: 15 minutes

---

1 pound ground beef

1 can (10 3/4 ounces) Campbell's® Condensed Bean with Bacon Soup

1 cup Pace® Picante Sauce

8 flour tortillas (8-inch), warmed

Shredded Cheddar cheese

Sour cream (optional)

1. Cook the beef in a 10-inch skillet over medium-high heat until it's well browned, stirring often to separate meat. Pour off any fat.

2. Stir the soup and picante sauce in the skillet and cook until the mixture is hot and bubbling, mashing the beans with a fork.

3. Spoon *about 1/2 cup* beef mixture down the center of *each* tortilla. Top with the cheese, additional picante sauce and sour cream, if desired. Fold the tortillas around the filling.

Spicy Grilled Quesadillas

Makes 4 servings

Prep Time: 10 minutes   Cook Time: 5 minutes   Stand Time: 2 minutes

8   flour tortillas (8-inch)

2   cups shredded Cheddar cheese (about 8 ounces)

1   jar (16 ounces) Pace® Picante Sauce

1   cup diced cooked chicken

4   medium green onions, chopped (about $1/2$ cup)

   Vegetable oil

1   container (8 ounces) sour cream

1. Top **each** of **4** tortillas with **$1/2$ cup** cheese, **$1/4$ cup** picante sauce, **$1/4$ cup** chicken and **2 tablespoons** green onions. Brush the edges of the tortillas with water. Top with the remaining tortillas and press the edges to seal.

2. Lightly oil the grill rack and heat the grill to medium. Brush the tops of the quesadillas with oil. Place the quesadillas, oil-side down, on the grill rack. Brush the other side of the quesadillas with oil. Grill the quesadillas for 5 minutes or until the cheese is melted, turning the quesadillas over once during grilling. Remove the quesadillas from the grill and let stand 2 minutes.

3. Cut the quesadillas into wedges. Serve with the remaining picante sauce and sour cream.

Kitchen Tip

Quesadillas are an easy way to turn leftover meat and shredded cheese into a whole new meal. You can even combine different varieties of shredded cheese to make the 2 cups needed in this recipe.

Classic Campbelled Eggs

Makes 4 servings

Prep Time: 5 minutes   Cook Time: 15 minutes

1 can (10³/₄ ounces) Campbell's® Condensed Cream of Celery Soup (Regular *or* 98% Fat Free)

8 eggs

Dash ground black pepper

2 tablespoons butter

Chopped fresh parsley

1. Beat the soup, eggs and black pepper in a medium bowl with a fork or whisk.

2. Heat the butter in a 10-inch skillet over low heat. Add the egg mixture and cook until the eggs are set but still moist. Garnish with the parsley.

Kitchen Tip

You can substitute Campbell's® Condensed Cheddar Cheese Soup for the Cream of Celery.

Turkey & Tortellini Alfredo

Makes 6 servings

Prep Time: 5 minutes   Cook Time: 15 minutes

- 1 pound Italian-style turkey sausage, casing removed
- 1 can (10 3/4 ounces) Campbell's® Condensed Cream of Chicken Soup (Regular *or* 98% Fat Free)
- 1/2 cup water
- 1 can (14.5 ounces) diced tomatoes, undrained
- 1 pound frozen cheese-filled tortellini
- 2 tablespoons chopped fresh basil leaves

  Grated Parmesan cheese (optional)

1. Cook the sausage in a 10-inch skillet over medium-high heat until it's well browned, stirring frequently to separate meat. Pour off any fat.

2. Stir the soup, water and tomatoes with juice into the skillet. Heat to a boil. Add the tortellini and reduce the heat to low. Cook for about 5 minutes or until the tortellini is tender but still firm.

3. Stir in the basil. Serve with cheese, if desired.

Fontina Turkey Panini

Makes 2 sandwiches

Prep Time: 5 minutes   Cook Time: 10 minutes

- 4 slices Pepperidge Farm® Farmhouse Sourdough Bread

   Olive oil

- 2 tablespoons honey mustard salad dressing

- 4 slices fontina cheese

- 2 slices smoked turkey

- 4 bread-and-butter pickle sandwich slices

1. Brush one side of the bread slices with the oil.

2. Turn **2** bread slices oil-side down. Spread **each** with **1 tablespoon** salad dressing. Top **each** with **2** cheese slices, **1** turkey slice, **2** pickle slices and the remaining bread slices, oil-side up.

3. Heat a grill pan or skillet over medium heat. Add the sandwiches and cook for 4 minutes or until they're lightly browned on both sides and the cheese is melted.

Kitchen Tip

Try pressing down on the sandwiches with a spatula during cooking. It will help the different ingredients melt together.

20-Minute Seafood Stew

Makes 4 servings

Prep Time: 5 minutes   Cook Time: 15 minutes

2 cups Prego® Traditional Italian Sauce

1 bottle (8 ounces) clam juice

1/4 cup Burgundy *or* other dry red wine (optional)

1 pound fresh *or* thawed frozen fish *and/or* shellfish*

8 small clams

Chopped fresh parsley

Use any one or a combination of the following: firm white fish fillets (cut into 2-inch pieces), boneless fish steaks (cut into 1-inch cubes), medium shrimp (peeled and deveined) or scallops.

1. Heat the Italian sauce, clam juice and wine, if desired, in a 4-quart saucepan over medium heat to a boil. Reduce the heat to low. Cook for 5 minutes.

2. Stir the fish and clams in the saucepan. Cover and cook for 5 minutes or until the fish and clams are done. Garnish with the parsley.

Kitchen Tip

Before cooking, discard any clams that remain open when tapped. After cooking, discard any clams that remain closed.

Fettuccine Picante

Makes 4 servings

Prep Time: 15 minutes   Cook Time: 5 minutes

- 1/2 cup Pace® Picante Sauce
- 1/2 cup sour cream
- 1/3 cup grated Parmesan cheese
- 1/2 of a 1-pound package fettuccine, cooked and drained
- 2 tablespoons chopped fresh cilantro leaves

1. Heat the picante sauce, sour cream and cheese in a 2-quart saucepan over medium heat until the mixture is hot and bubbling.

2. Place the fettuccine and cilantro into a large serving bowl. Add the mixture and toss to coat. Serve with additional picante sauce.

Kitchen Tip

*You can use Pace® mild, medium **or** hot Picante Sauce in this recipe.*

Cheese Steak Pockets

Makes 8 sandwiches

Prep Time: 5 minutes   Cook Time: 10 minutes

---

1 tablespoon vegetable oil

1 medium onion, sliced

1 package (14 ounces) frozen beef *or* chicken sandwich steaks, separated into 8 portions

1 can (10$^3/_4$ ounces) Campbell's® Condensed Cheddar Cheese Soup

1 jar (about 4$^1/_2$ ounces) sliced mushrooms, drained

4 pita breads (6-inch), cut in half

1. Heat the oil in a 10-inch skillet over medium-high heat. Add the onion. Cook and stir until the onion is tender.

2. Add the sandwich steaks and cook until they're browned. Pour off any fat.

3. Add the soup and mushrooms. Reduce the heat to low. Cook and stir until the mixture is hot and bubbling.

4. Divide and spoon the meat mixture into the pita halves.

Breakfast Tacos

Makes 2 servings

Prep Time: 10 minutes   Cook Time: 10 minutes

- 1 tablespoon butter
- 1 cup diced cooked potato
- 4 eggs, beaten
- 4 slices bacon, cooked and crumbled
- 4 flour tortillas (8-inch), warmed
- $3/4$ cup shredded Cheddar cheese
- $1/2$ cup Pace® Picante Sauce

1. Heat the butter in a 10-inch skillet over medium heat. Add the potato and cook until it's lightly browned, stirring often. Stir in the eggs and bacon and cook until the eggs are set, stirring often.

2. Spoon *about $1/2$ cup* potato mixture down the center of *each* tortilla. Divide the cheese and picante sauce evenly among the tortillas. Fold the tortillas around the filling.

Shredded Chicken Soft Tacos

Makes 8 tacos

Prep Time: 5 minutes   Cook Time: 10 minutes

1 jar (16 ounces) Pace® Picante Sauce

3 cups shredded cooked chicken

8 flour tortillas (8-inch), warmed

   Guacamole

   Chopped tomatoes

   Fresh cilantro leaves (optional)

1. Heat the picante sauce and chicken in a 2-quart saucepan over medium heat until the mixture is hot and bubbling, stirring often.

2. Spoon **about ⅓ cup** chicken mixture down the center of **each** tortilla. Top with the guacamole, tomatoes and cilantro, if desired. Fold the tortillas around the filling.

Kitchen Tip

Use store-bought rotisserie chicken or refrigerated cooked chicken strips, shredded, for this recipe.

Picante Skillet Chicken

Makes 6 servings

Prep Time: 5 minutes   Cook Time: 15 minutes

1 tablespoon vegetable oil

1¹/₂ pounds skinless, boneless chicken breast halves (4 to 6)

1 jar (16 ounces) Pace® Picante Sauce

6 cups hot cooked regular long-grain white rice

1. Heat the oil in a 10-inch skillet over medium-high heat. Add the chicken and cook for 10 minutes or until it's well browned on both sides.

2. Add the picante sauce to the skillet. Heat to a boil. Reduce the heat to medium. Cover and cook for 5 minutes or until the chicken is cooked through.

3. Serve with the rice.

Italian Sausage Sandwiches

Makes 4 sandwiches

Prep Time: 5 minutes   Cook Time: 15 minutes

---

   1 pound Italian pork sausage, casing removed

1½ cups Prego® Chunky Garden Mushroom & Green Pepper Italian Sauce

   4 long hard rolls, split

1. Cook the sausage in a 10-inch skillet over medium-high heat until it's well browned, stirring often to separate meat. Pour off any fat.

2. Stir in the Italian sauce and cook until the mixture is hot and bubbling. Serve the sausage mixture on the rolls.

Kitchen Tip

You can use your favorite Prego® Italian Sauce in this recipe.

Baked Potatoes Olé

Makes 4 servings

Prep Time: 5 minutes   Cook Time: 15 minutes

- 1 pound ground beef
- 1 tablespoon chili powder
- 1 cup Pace® Picante Sauce
- 4 hot baked potatoes, split

  Shredded Cheddar cheese

1. Cook the beef and chili powder in a 10-inch skillet over medium-high heat until the beef is well browned, stirring often to separate meat. Pour off any fat.

2. Stir the picante sauce in the skillet. Reduce the heat to low. Cook until the mixture is hot and bubbling. Serve the beef mixture over the potatoes. Top with the cheese.

Kitchen Tip

To bake the potatoes, pierce them with a fork and bake at 400°F. for 1 hour or microwave on HIGH for 12 minutes or until fork-tender.

Cheesy Broccoli Potato Topper

Makes 4 servings

Prep Time: 10 minutes   Cook Time: 4 minutes

1 can (10$^3/_4$ ounces) Campbell's® Condensed Cheddar Cheese Soup

4 hot baked potatoes, split

1 cup cooked broccoli flowerets

1. Stir the soup in the can until it's smooth.

2. Place the potatoes onto a microwavable plate. Top with the broccoli. Spoon the soup over the broccoli.

3. Microwave on HIGH for 4 minutes or until the soup is hot.

Quick Chicken Mozzarella Sandwiches

Makes 4 sandwiches

Prep Time: 5 minutes   Cook Time: 15 minutes

1¹/₂ cups Prego® Three Cheese Italian Sauce

  4 refrigerated *or* thawed frozen cooked breaded chicken cutlets

  4 slices mozzarella cheese

  4 round hard rolls

1. Heat the Italian sauce in a 10-inch skillet over medium heat to a boil. Place the chicken in the sauce. Reduce the heat to low. Cover and cook for 5 minutes or until the chicken is heated through.

2. Top the chicken with the cheese. Cover and cook until the cheese is melted. Serve on the rolls.

Apple & Cheddar Bagel Melt Sandwiches

Makes 4 sandwiches

Prep Time: 5 minutes   Broil Time: 2 minutes

- ¼ cup honey
- 4 Pepperidge Farm® Sesame Bagels, split and toasted *or* Pepperidge Farm® Onion Bagels, split and toasted
- 1 medium Granny Smith apple, thinly sliced
- 4 slices Cheddar cheese

1. Heat the broiler. Spread the honey among the bagel halves. Place **4** bagel halves onto a baking sheet and top with the apple and cheese.

2. Broil the bagels with the tops of the bagels 4 inches from the heat for 2 minutes or until the cheese is melted.

3. Top with the remaining bagel halves. Serve immediately.

Kitchen Tip

*Substitute **12** Pepperidge Farm® Mini Bagels, any variety, for the regular-size bagels.*

Asian Chicken Stir-Fry

Makes 4 servings

Prep Time: 5 minutes   Cook Time: 15 minutes

- 1 tablespoon vegetable oil
- 1 pound skinless, boneless chicken breasts, cut into strips
- 1 can (10 3/4 ounces) Campbell's® Condensed Golden Mushroom Soup
- 3 tablespoons soy sauce
- 1 teaspoon garlic powder
- 1 bag (16 ounces) any frozen vegetable combination
- Hot cooked rice

1. Heat the oil in a 10-inch skillet over medium-high heat. Add the chicken and stir-fry until it's well browned.

2. Stir the soup, soy sauce and garlic powder into the skillet. Heat to a boil. Add the vegetables. Cook and stir until vegetables are tender-crisp. Serve over the rice.

Hearty Ham and Onion Melts

Makes 2 sandwiches

Prep Time: 5 minutes   Cook Time: 15 minutes

Vegetable cooking spray

1 small red onion, thinly sliced

3 tablespoons balsamic vinegar

4 slices Pepperidge Farm® 100% Natural Honey Flax Bread

2 ounces deli-sliced reduced-sodium ham

2 ounces sliced Muenster cheese *or* provolone cheese

1. Spray a 10-inch skillet with the cooking spray and heat over medium heat for 1 minute. Add the onions and cook until they begin to soften. Add the vinegar and cook for 2 minutes or until the onions are tender.

2. Top **2** bread slices with the ham, cheese, onion mixture and remaining bread slices.

3. Spray the skillet with the cooking spray and heat over medium heat for 1 minute. Add the sandwiches and cook until they're lightly browned on both sides and the cheese is melted.

Kitchen Tip

Also delicious with Pepperidge Farm® 100% Natural German Dark Wheat Bread.

Chicken Broccoli Pockets

Makes 6 sandwiches

Prep Time: 15 minutes   Cook Time: 5 minutes

- 1 can (10 3/4 ounces) Campbell's® Healthy Request® Condensed Cream of Chicken Soup
- 1/4 cup water
- 1 tablespoon lemon juice
- 1/4 teaspoon garlic powder
- 1/8 teaspoon ground black pepper
- 1 cup cooked broccoli flowerets
- 1 medium carrot, shredded (about 1/2 cup)
- 2 cups cubed cooked chicken *or* turkey
- 3 pita breads (6-inch), cut in half, forming 2 pockets

1. Heat all the ingredients, except pita breads, in a 2-quart saucepan over medium heat until the mixture is hot and bubbling.

2. Spoon the chicken mixture into the pita pockets.

Kitchen Tip

This chicken mixture is also delicious served over hot baked potatoes.

Herb Grilled Vegetables

Makes 6 servings

Prep Time: 10 minutes   Cook Time: 10 minutes

1/2 cup Swanson® Natural Goodness® Chicken Broth

1/2 teaspoon dried thyme leaves, crushed

1/8 teaspoon ground black pepper

  1 large red onion, thickly sliced (about 1 cup)

  1 large red *or* green pepper, cut into wide strips (about 2 cups)

  1 medium zucchini *or* yellow squash, thickly sliced (about 1 1/2 cups)

  2 cups large mushrooms

1. Stir the broth, thyme and black pepper in a small bowl. Brush the vegetables with the broth mixture.

2. Lightly oil the grill rack and heat the grill to medium. Grill the vegetables for 10 minutes or until they're tender-crisp, turning over once during cooking and brushing often with the broth mixture.

Kitchen Tip

A grilling basket is handy for grilling smaller foods like these veggies. Just place the vegetables in a single layer in the basket, close and place on the grill. You can baste the vegetables right in the basket, and flip the basket to grill the other side.

Swanson® Vegetable Broth may be used instead of Swanson® Chicken Broth for a vegetarian dish.

Tuna Niçoise Sandwiches

Makes 2 sandwiches

Prep Time: 10 minutes

- 2 tablespoons mayonnaise
- 2 tablespoons Dijon-style mustard
- 1 can (6 ounces) low-sodium chunk white tuna packed in water, drained
- 1 green onion, sliced (about 2 tablespoons)
- 1 tablespoon pitted, chopped kalamata olives
- 1 tablespoon drained capers
- 4 slices Pepperidge Farm® Whole Grain 100% Whole Wheat Bread
  Red leaf lettuce leaves

1. Stir the mayonnaise and mustard in a medium bowl. Stir in the tuna, onion, olives and capers.

2. Divide the tuna mixture between **2** bread slices. Top with the lettuce and remaining bread slices.

Banana-Stuffed French Toast

Makes 2 servings

Prep Time: 10 minutes   Cook Time: 10 minutes

- $^1/_2$ cup cholesterol-free egg substitute
- $^1/_2$ cup nonfat milk
- $^1/_4$ teaspoon vanilla extract
- 4 slices Pepperidge Farm® 100% Natural 100% Whole Wheat Bread
  Vegetable cooking spray
- 1 medium banana, sliced
  Cinnamon-sugar
- 1 cup fresh blueberries
- $^1/_2$ cup maple-flavored syrup

1. Beat the egg substitute, milk and vanilla in a 2-quart shallow baking dish with a fork or whisk. Add the bread slices and turn to coat. Let stand for about 4 minutes.

2. Spray a 12-inch skillet with the cooking spray and heat over medium heat for 1 minute. Add the bread slices and cook until they're lightly browned on both sides.

3. Place **1** toast on a serving plate. Top with **half** the banana and another toast. Sprinkle with the cinnamon-sugar and **$^1/_2$ cup** blueberries. Repeat with the remaining ingredients. Serve with the syrup.

Kitchen Tip

To make the cinnamon-sugar, stir **1 tablespoon** sugar and $^1/_2$ **tablespoon** cinnamon in a small bowl.

Bruschetta Salad

Makes 6 servings

Prep Time: 20 minutes

- ¹/₂ cup olive oil
- 2 tablespoons red wine vinegar
- 2 medium tomatoes, cut into 1-inch pieces (about 2 cups)
- ¹/₂ cup thinly sliced cucumber
- 1 medium red onion, thinly sliced (about ¹/₂ cup)
- ¹/₄ cup chopped fresh basil leaves
- 1 tablespoon drained capers
- 2 cups Pepperidge Farm® Whole Grain Seasoned Croutons

1. Beat the oil and vinegar in a large bowl with a fork or whisk until blended. Add the tomatoes, cucumber, onion, basil and capers and toss to coat. Season to taste.

2. Add the croutons just before serving and toss to coat. Serve immediately.

Kitchen Tip

It's important to serve this salad immediately so that the croutons will stay crisp.

Fabulous Fast Shrimp

Makes 4 servings

Prep Time: 5 minutes   Cook Time: 15 minutes

- 1 tablespoon butter *or* margarine
- 2 stalks celery, chopped
- 1/4 cup chopped green pepper
- 1/4 cup sliced green onions
- 1 pound fresh large shrimp, shelled and deveined
- 1 can (10 3/4 ounces) Campbell's® Condensed Cream of Chicken Soup (Regular *or* 98% Fat Free)
- 1/2 cup water
  - Dash of cayenne pepper
  - Hot cooked rice
  - Paprika

1. Heat butter in skillet. Add celery, green pepper and green onions and cook until tender. Add shrimp and cook 3 to 5 minutes or until done.

2. Add soup, water and cayenne pepper and heat through.

3. Serve over rice. Sprinkle with paprika.